HERITAGE
style

Selina Lake

HERITAGE
style

A FRESH
NEW TAKE ON
TRADITIONAL
DESIGN

PHOTOGRAPHY BY
RACHEL WHITING

RYLAND PETERS & SMALL
LONDON • NEW YORK

Senior designer Megan Smith
Senior commissioning editor
Annabel Morgan
Location research Jess Walton
Production manager
Gordana Simakovic
Art director Leslie Harrington
Publisher Cindy Richards

First published in 2022 by
Ryland Peters & Small
20–21 Jockey's Fields
London WC1R 4BW
and
341 E 116th Street
New York, NY 10029

www.rylandpeters.com

Text copyright © Selina Lake 2022
Design and photographs copyright
© Ryland Peters & Small 2022

10 9 8 7 6 5 4 3 2 1

ISBN 978-1-78879-432-9

A CIP record for this book is available
from the British Library.

Library of Congress CIP data has been
applied for.

Printed and bound in China

MIX
Paper from
responsible sources
FSC® C106563

CONTENTS

Heritage INSPIRATIONS

A FRESH APPROACH
TO A CLASSIC STYLE

Heritage style describes the balance of period properties with modern-day life. I love the definition of the word 'heritage' from the *Oxford English Dictionary*: 'The history, traditions, buildings and objects that a country or society has had for many years and that are considered an important part of its character.' When I added the word 'style' to create the title of this book, I wanted to evoke a modern sense of nostalgia.

My inspiration derives mostly from unique old buildings that have one foot in the past and one stepping into the future. I love to see how the craftsmanship and decorative details have stood the test of time. Unfortunately, in the 20th century, many older properties were stripped of period details that were then seen as 'fussy' but are now highly sought after. If you own such a building, you may be considering how to restore it at the same time as making it relevant to today. Or perhaps you live in a new-build and are wondering how your inherited pieces will fit in?

Heritage style is all about preserving the past while incorporating your own heritage and personal style, in keeping with the character of your space. Research period architecture and heritage colours and patterns, or look to your surrounding area and its history. Every home is different, but I hope my take on heritage style, along with the designers and homeowners who have opened their doors for this book, will inspire you. Along the way, I will offer tips on what to celebrate in an older property together with ideas for colours, patterns and furniture with which to enrich your space.

PAST TO PRESENT
This hand-painted floral design on porcelain is a practice piece from the Coalport China Company founded by John Rose in 1795. It has been handed down and is now treasured by the artist and designer Elizabeth Rose (*above*). In his Georgian seaside cottage in Kent, artist Russell Loughlan has painted stripes on his bedroom walls (*right*). Classic furniture with stripes, florals and velvets make up this living-room scheme (*opposite*).

Heritage ELEMENTS

TIMELESS GARDENS

Outside spaces offer endless colour and design inspiration. If a garden is well stocked with flowers and foliage for cutting, these can also be brought inside to bring an interiors scheme to life. This lovely country garden in Kent features intriguing pathways and romantic planting, with an element of interest around every corner (*opposite*). The grand Victorian architecture of this London house has been softened with roses and rambling wisteria (*above*). Yellow mustard plant flowers brighten up a kitchen (*above right*). These freshly picked summer blooms are ready to fill a room with colour and scent (*right*).

NATURE AS MUSE

You only have to look at my Instagram feed (@selinalake) to know that I have a great love of the natural world and I really wanted this book to reference designers of the past who took their inspiration directly from nature. This hallway in Bella and Hugo Middleton's Georgian manor in Lincolnshire features a classic Honeysuckle wallpaper designed by William Morris's daughter May for Morris & Co. in 1883 (*opposite and above*). Bella has echoed the design by placing vases of fresh flowers on all available surfaces. The bench has cushions in a mix of floral and striped fabrics. Meanwhile, in an Arts and Crafts house, antique plates with stylized floral and fauna patterns in cobalt blue have been used to adorn the space above a fireplace mantel (*left*).

ARCHITECTURAL ELEMENTS

The bones of a house.

People often talk about a property having 'good bones' and this usually means it is rich in original features, with good light and well-sized rooms. If you're lucky enough to live in such a home, let your styling be led by the architecture and original colours and materials of the building, while in a modern home or one that has lost such features, you can draw inspiration from the architecture of your village, town or street. In this section, I take a look at some of the architectural features that contribute to the heritage look and suggest how you might be able to reinstate or replicate them without your interior looking like a pastiche or something from a period drama. Such elements are lovely, but they are not key to heritage style. You can use colour, furniture, fabrics and art to create the style, so don't despair if your home doesn't have those elusive 'good bones' – the look is still within reach.

PAST GLORIES
This elegant dining room in a Victorian townhouse on the coast is a heritage-lover's dream, from the original floorboards up to the intricate early Victorian ceiling mouldings and marble chimneypiece (*right*).

period features

Celebrating original elements starts by preserving the architectural details of which you have become a custodian when buying or renting a period property. These may include old pine floorboards, attractive plaster cornices/crown moldings, wooden ceiling beams, decorative 19th-century tiles and pretty fireplaces. Original features such as these will give an instant injection of heritage style, even if they need a bit of restoration or a coat of paint.

But what if you live in a different kind of home – one where all the period charm has been ruthlessly ripped out, or in a new-build house or modern apartment? The good news is that it's possible to reproduce these kinds of features in your space. Salvage is the best option, partly because salvaged items are more sustainable as well as looking authentic, but if you don't have time or are not able to find suitable reclaimed examples, wooden wall panelling or tongue and groove can be bought by the metre/yard from DIY/hardware stores and specialist suppliers. There are multiple fireplace companies offering period styles, but if you're on a budget, look at online auction sites – that's where I sourced our living room fire surround.

HERITAGE DETAILS

A beech branch in a stoneware vase brings alive this mantelpiece, with the mirror behind doubling the effect of the foliage (*opposite left*). If you are lucky enough to uncover an original feature like this tiled hearth, make the most of it by using it as the inspiration for a decorative scheme, picking out patterns or colours to repeat elsewhere in the space (*opposite right*). Thickly lined slubby linen curtains complement the decorative mouldings and work hard to keep draughts at bay (*above left*). A simple yet beautiful mahogany antique table is the perfect addition to this hallway (*above*).

When it comes to flooring, sourcing salvaged boards makes perfect sense and nowadays there are many companies that offer 'new' old flooring, as well as new flooring that looks old. You may also want to bring a sense of history sympathetically by adding decorative plaster details such as ceiling roses or cornicing/crown moldings, or build in cabinetry with classic styling. Even attaching traditional-style knobs or handles to your kitchen cabinets or front door will bring a heritage flavour, as will choosing the right paint colours – ones that evoke a sense of comfort, familiarity and warmth.

This impressive headboard was created by Jessie Cutts and Ivo Vos from architectural salvage left in the property by the previous owner, who was an antiques dealer. Possibly once a section of wall panelling, the piece isn't original to their property, but it just goes to show that items don't always have to be truly authentic to work (*above left*).

something about salvage

The heritage look doesn't have to be grand – it can hark back to humble homes too, where craftsmanship and care were taken to build practical features into any everyday space. From doorways and built-in cupboards to window shutters, these original elements deserve to be cherished. If your property doesn't possess many interesting features, you can add your own – salvaged materials will instantly add texture and character. Paint can be used to give the impression of high ceilings by continuing the wall colour up and across the ceiling. Adapt architectural finds to fit your ideas, making unique headboards from sections of wooden panelling and cladding walls with reclaimed boarding, for example. The good news is these found items don't necessarily need to be authentic to the age and style of your home – just make sure you choose ones that are in keeping with the overall feel you're creating.

PERFECT PAIRING

In Elizabeth Rose's bedroom, salvaged cladding with a rich patina is accented with a sage green door, while exposed ceiling beams and an earthy red fireplace create a homely, rustic mood. The room is given a boho twist by simply hanging a favourite garment on the door (*this page and opposite right*).

WONDERFUL WINDOWS

Window treatments can be minimal when the frames are this attractive, although old single-glazed windows are notorious for being draughty so it might be an idea to have a curtain plan for the winter months. The half-moon fanlight window above these French doors adds an architectural element as well as extra light (*above*). This Georgian sash window with built-in shutters and seat is the perfect spot to look over the garden below (*above right*). Adding a splash of colour to a window frame is designer Elizabeth Rose's signature look (*right*). A generous curved bay window painted in the most perfect shade of sea green allows light to flood this playroom (*opposite*).

Add Character

When it comes to choosing a colour palette, seek out brands that offer a range of shades that hark back to yesteryear. Such muted, elegant colours give displays and accessories a subtle yet beautiful backdrop.

REPLACING LOST FEATURES
The Victorian mantelpiece was long gone when we moved into our house; all that remained was a hole in the wall and a stone hearth. I found this marble mantelpiece on an online auction site, and even though it wasn't exactly the right size, my husband Dave and I decided to buy it. Dave is a DIY enthusiast with expert skills to match, so he set about cutting the marble and slate surround to fit. It totally made the room when it was installed and has given me a place for ever-changing seasonal styling opportunities.

MAKE A STATEMENT
The addition of a wooden shelf and chunky brackets gives this small fireplace more presence (*left*). Designer Sophie Rowell used Filthy Terracotta from The Pickleson Paint Co. to give her mantelpiece a new look. I like the way she has taken the paint up the wall to create more impact (*above*).

fireplaces – a central focus

I'm a firm believer that a fireplace can make a room. They work in all types of property and can be purely decorative or an integral part of a home heating system. As a stylist, it is the mantelpiece surrounding the fireplace that I find the most appealing – it is the perfect spot for a styling moment and anything goes really, from flowers, candles, mirrors and clocks to vintage metal toys, decorative ceramics and straw hats. If you have inherited or installed an open fireplace or wood-burning stove without a mantelpiece to style, try hanging a thick shelf, or make the most of the area around it, adding logs, kindling and fireside accessories in baskets or little wooden stools for lanterns and candles. I use a vintage wire potato basket to store kindling along with baskets for logs. All the original fireplaces in our Victorian house were absent when we moved in, so slowly we have been sourcing salvaged examples to reinstate.

traditional panelling & joinery

Heritage homes are places that deliver functionality and elegance, and decorative joinery is an integral part of the picture. Think tailored cabinetry for storage, wall panelling and partition walls with internal windows that flood light into an interior. Panelling was traditionally used to provide insulation, but nowadays it's mainly added as decoration. New homes can be fitted with panelling either as feature walls or as fully fitted rooms; commission a carpenter for something custom-made or take a look at The English Panelling Company for bespoke designs that you can fit yourself. Joinery can give a room personality and equip it for its function – boot rooms, for example, feature built-in benches and shelves with hooks for hanging outerwear, bags and hats, plus storage below for boots, of course. Half-panelled walls work particularly well in utility rooms, bathrooms and cloakrooms – paint them with soft sheen or gloss so that they can be cleaned easily.

DECORATIVE EFFECTS

A bold scheme using Farrow & Ball paints gives this hallway the wow factor (*above left*). An en-suite bathroom tucked behind a part-glazed timber partition ensures no natural light is lost (*above*). Some of the original panelling was damaged in the dining room of this Georgian house, so owner Russell Loughlan commissioned a local carpenter to replicate and replace it (*opposite*).

TIMELESS COLOUR & PATTERN

For a fresh, modern feel.

Colour and pattern are key elements of heritage style and there is a huge range of heritage paint colours as well as wallpaper and fabric patterns to choose from, with many companies looking to the past and historical properties for inspiration. Others have reproduced classic wallpaper designs and relaunched historic colours for use in modern-day homes. Heritage paint ranges tend to be fairly classic (you won't find an acid lime green or neon pink), meaning they work within a wide variety of settings. They can be grouped into four categories: whites, which tend to be off-whites with warm undertones; pale tones, consisting of soft, grown-up pastels; mid-tones, which are easy on the eye, slightly muted and used to create cosy spaces; and finally deep tones, which are rich and dramatic. There is something to suit all spaces in period or new properties.

EXQUISITE EMBELLISHMENT

Classic tongue-and-groove half-wall panelling painted in a soft green shade plus Topiary wallpaper in Leaf Green by Cole & Son is a smart and timeless combination (*opposite left*). Hand-painted antique glass can be used for internal windows or partitions, adding embellishment and allowing light into dark rooms (*opposite right*). Painting the simple wooden fire surround an earthy red brings a French farmhouse feel to a small bedroom (*above left*). This ornate wooden mantelpiece was painted to match Great Vine wallpaper by Cole & Son in the Aqua colourway (*above*).

Traditional wallpaper patterns, which were frequently inspired by nature, are often block printed in the same way now as when they were first produced. Classic designs, such as checks and stripes, are eternally popular, with gingham and wide stripes being particularly on trend at present. And the modern process of digital printing allows historic works of art to be reproduced as wallpaper or murals, converting tapestries and paintings into affordable yet timeless wall coverings.

Clay, plaster and powder pink tones are soft colours, used in any room in the house to add warmth and a subtle, grown-up elegance. These pastelly, earthy neutrals work perfectly in a heritage home, and combine well with deep reds, muted mustards and rich ambers. A soft and pretty putty pink tone gives a relaxing vibe in this bedroom, with rust-coloured and ticking striped linens dressing the bed (*left*). Amber pharmacy bottles bring a deeper tone to a wall painted plaster pink (*below left*). A built-in banquette in Sarah Brown's kitchen is painted a rich burgundy and teamed with butter yellow painted stools (*below*). A plaster pink colour covers the doorway, door frame and Georgian panelling in this living room (*opposite*). The gold silk sofa reflects the natural tones of golden sandstone and harmonizes with the walls and cushions.

soft pinks & earthy tones

Add Character

Colour inspiration can be sparked when samples of wallpaper, fabric and paint are all gathered together so that you can see at a glance how a colour scheme will work. The sources are listed on page 175.

If in doubt, go for green – after all, it's the colour of nature. Fresh greens combined with warm yellows will create a pretty, fresh feeling, especially when used in conjunction with untreated woods, natural fibre rugs and washed linens. Sarah Brown's cloakroom features a wraparound shelf, peg rail and built-in bench all painted in a hazy yellow (*left*). A scattering of ochre and mustard cushions works in harmony with leafy greens on our garden sofa (*below left*). A vintage milk bottle filled with dried leaves sits alongside a landscape painted by my late grandpa Ronald Lake, which has pride of place on our bedroom mantelpiece (*below*). Elizabeth Rose has used Green Verditer by Little Greene to add a pop of colour on her kitchen door and window (*opposite*).

fresh greens & ochre

OBJECTS OF DESIRE

Use treasured artworks and artefacts as the basis for a colour scheme. Here, warm earthy neutrals and rich celadon green provided me with inspiration for the moodboard opposite.

These cooler tones again come direct from Mother Nature, recalling the sea and the sky. Blues and greens are calming, so have been used to decorate bedrooms and bathrooms for centuries. Pair rich aqua with soft marine greens to create the liberating feeling of open skies and calm water. Anaglypta wallpaper with an Art Deco motif has been painted a soft sage green and teamed with mid-century plates, a metal bed frame and an Anglepoise lamp to bring a modern edge to this guest bedroom (*opposite*). A brighter blue the shade of the summer sky is appropriate for a bedroom that's so close to the beach you can almost hear the waves (*below*). Designed by talented muralist Flora Roberts, Alhambra wallpaper by Lewis & Wood is based on a Middle Eastern carpet (*below right*). A small-scale paper by Soane is ideal for adding character to both modern and historic interiors (*above right*).

rich blues
& sea greens

Add Character

Blues and greens make a great backdrop for a layered look. Add a vintage rug in rich red and antique brown furniture. Don't forget flowers – here, dusky pink hydrangeas are arranged in a blue and white pot.

Furnishing a heritage home is all about getting the right balance of old and new and blending pieces from different eras, and this tends to work best when items are tonally united. Lightweight rattan armchairs in their natural hue combined with a wooden chest with a scraped paint patina come together well with their warm neutral tones sitting comfortably against an unpainted plaster backdrop. The retro sunflower painting fits right in (*opposite*). Old armchairs and sofas with good shape can be kept as they are or covered in new fabrics to refresh their appearance (*left*).

FURNITURE
Confidently combining old & new.

Antiques were built to last, which is why so many pieces have survived to tell the tale. Opting for antique and vintage furniture is a sustainable way to furnish a home, as it has already been made so doesn't require valuable raw materials or resources to be produced and shipped. Retro furniture from the 1950s to 1970s is very on trend. Look out for mid-century armchairs, sideboards and tables at car boot/yard sales and vintage fairs – they are often neat in size and shape, so perfect for modern homes. So-called brown furniture is making a comeback and sturdy 19th- and early 20th-century pieces are desirable again. Look for bobbin furniture, campaign chests or items with scalloped detailing. Great craftsmanship stands the test of time, so it's no surprise these articles are being celebrated again.

take a seat

A comfy chair is perhaps the most used and valued piece of furniture in the home, and iconic designs of the past still provide inspiration to makers today. Think of classic Windsor chairs, wingback armchairs, Hans J Wegner's Wishbone chair and Chesterfield sofas. Antique examples are not without their challenges, as period furniture will probably at some point require reupholstering or repairing and the materials must be maintained, especially wood and leather, which can need feeding, waxing or polishing. As with most things, seating styles come in and out of fashion, and right now bobbin furniture, rattan chairs and benches, wood and leather safari chairs and classic Howard-style sofas and armchairs are all on trend. Armchairs can be positioned in generous-sized hallways and bathrooms as well as living spaces and bedrooms. An ideal spot is next to a fireplace or in front of a window so that you can take a moment to yourself and enjoy the view.

PULL UP A CHAIR

The way seating is arranged can change the feel of a room from stiff and formal to warm and welcoming. Antique armchairs sit invitingly either side of a bedroom fireplace (*above left*). A retro safari chair is positioned to overlook a London garden (*above*). A French tub chair upholstered in duck egg blue linen looks even more comfy with the addition of a gingham cushion (*opposite*).

Future Heritage

Seek out chairs made with the craftsmanship and skills of yesteryear, and constructed from quality planet-friendly materials. Such pieces will weave themselves into the homes of the future.

SOPHISTICATED SEATS

This London living room designed by Anna Haines benefits from a collection of seating opportunities, making it a great social space. A deep sofa faces the fireplace with a pair of chairs positioned in the bay window upholstered in an elegant woven fabric called Sophia by Susan Deliss. An upholstered footstool acts as a generous coffee table and displays piles of favourite books (*opposite*). Anna has positioned a low spindle-back mid-century armchair beside the fireplace and against walls and a built-in bookcase painted in Farrow & Ball's French Gray (*right*).

RELAX & RECLINE

This double-aspect spot seems the perfect place for a daybed covered in an off-white bouclé wool fabric and dressed with a Tulips of Belgravia cushion by Ottoline. A flash of blue from a side table designed by Sarah Brown sits alongside (*above*). This generous hallway belonging to Jessie Cutts and Ivo Vos boasts space for an antique country bench with woven rush seats (*opposite*).

CUSTOM-BUILT BEAUTY

Once you've found a long-term home, commissioning a carpenter to build storage to perfectly fit into the contours of your property will make the best use of the available space. Genevieve Harris designed these floor-to-ceiling kitchen cupboards to give her kitchen a farmhouse look; she chose a happy yellow colour and finished the doors with brass knobs (*left and opposite*). You may be lucky enough to find something antique that looks as though it was made to fit, like this huge floor-to-ceiling unit that covers a wall in the dining room of Jessie Cutts and Ivo Vos (*below*).

a place for everything

Having a well-organized home engenders a sense of harmony and calm, and custom-made built-in or freestanding cupboards are excellent options for kitchen and dining-room storage. These additions don't have to blend into the walls either; you could paint them in a jolly tone. Heritage style is about creating a classic, timeless and easy-to-live-with home, and hard-working storage solutions keep everything in check. Obviously clutter can look great and bring lots of character to rooms, but storing away those items that are essential yet less appealing to look at will make the lucky ones that get to stay out on display even more special. Second-hand chests of drawers, bookcases and dressers/hutches are all good options. If you plump for second-hand, just make sure you store heavier items at the bottom of the piece to add weight and prevent it from toppling over.

TABLE TALK

Designer Anna Haines' kitchen has a large family-sized table in the centre of the space, and the clever combination of mid-century chairs with a long bench running along one side feels informal while still being sophisticated (*opposite*). An antique dark wood table sits on herringbone flooring in designer Sophie Rowell's home. The wooden chairs are mismatched and the pretty antique ceramic chandelier enjoys pride of place (*right*).

around the table

When I think about dining tables, my mind conjures up a family meeting point with lively conversations, great meals and plenty of space for craft projects, puzzles and baking. Tables can be investment pieces that can see you through various homes. If you're renting or currently have a small dining room, choose tables that have been cleverly made to extend to future-proof them. I'm a firm believer that any table can be elevated with a tablecloth and right now I'm loving ones that feature ruffled or scalloped edging. When styling tables for special meals, I like to use linen napkins and place flowers or foliage in vases to decorate the table. A set of dining chairs can be expensive if new and if buying antique it's rare to find a set of, say, six or eight matching chairs that are all in good condition. The budget-friendly option is to collect chairs in different styles and opt for an eclectic look rather than being matchy-matchy.

Once you've found a long-term home, commissioning a carpenter to build storage to perfectly fit into the contours of your property will make the best use of the available space. Genevieve Harris designed these floor-to-ceiling kitchen cupboards to give her kitchen a farmhouse look; she chose a happy yellow colour and finished the doors with brass knobs (*left and opposite*). You may be lucky enough to find something antique that looks as though it was made to fit, like this huge floor-to-ceiling unit that covers a wall in the dining room of Jessie Cutts and Ivo Vos (*below*).

a place for everything

Having a well-organized home engenders a sense of harmony and calm, and custom-made built-in or freestanding cupboards are excellent options for kitchen and dining-room storage. These additions don't have to blend into the walls either; you could paint them in a jolly tone. Heritage style is about creating a classic, timeless and easy-to-live-with home, and hard-working storage solutions keep everything in check. Obviously clutter can look great and bring lots of character to rooms, but storing away those items that are essential yet less appealing to look at will make the lucky ones that get to stay out on display even more special. Second-hand chests of drawers, bookcases and dressers/hutches are all good options. If you plump for second-hand, just make sure you store heavier items at the bottom of the piece to add weight and prevent it from toppling over.

WOOD WORKS

From chests of drawers to farmhouse dressers/ hutches to industrial trolleys, wooden storage is a good choice for a heritage-style home as it's so durable. A slightly battered Georgian linen press adds period charm to a bedroom (*above*). This elegant polished wooden chest of drawers tidies away bed linen (*above right*). A rustic two-part dresser/hutch with tongue-and-groove doors below and glass doors above houses a collection of antique china (*right*), while an industrial trolley has become an integral part of this kitchen and puts everyday items within easy reach (*opposite*).

DECORATIVE DETAILS

Decorative details & display.

Accessories, personal touches and eye-catching collectables are particularly important when creating a heritage home, and as a stylist this is one of my favourite ways to bring interest and atmosphere to a room. Creating displays and little vignettes using decorative and inherited pieces adds colour, texture and a sense of history to any interior. Perhaps you have already amassed a collection of items over the years, or you are just starting to gather. Either way, I would recommend having a root about at home before buying anything new and taking another look at objects that you might not have thought of as decorative before. You can gather together a selection of items that all share a particular colour, or perhaps find a different purpose for an object – water jugs/pitchers make great vases, for example, while plates look as good as paintings on the wall.

CREATIVE COMPOSITIONS

When it comes to display, tap into your creativity and explore different arrangements. A cluster of containers holding seasonal flowers and plants beautifies any mantelpiece (*opposite left*). A collection of vintage creamware plates and platters glazed in pale tones adds texture to a plain wall (*opposite right*). Lighting can be part of a display – place lamps with contrasting shades against strongly coloured walls or decorative wallpaper (*above left*). This careful grouping of stoneware adds a tactile, earthy feel to a stone mantelpiece (*above*).

Creating decorative displays can be as simple as placing a stack of attractive old books on a sideboard alongside a vase of flowers, or using a pretty tray to display a selection of candles and curios. I take a relaxed approach when sourcing new styling props to use at home – if I see a junk/antique/thrift or vintage shop when I'm out and about, I will always pop in for a browse, but I try to only buy things that I just can't leave behind, or which spark an idea for a new styling project.

displays

Period items that have been cherished or handed down through a family tell a story, and displaying these items in your home will add a sense of history. Use furniture, walls and open shelves to group items together. Well-considered displays bring personality to your space, but don't overthink it – our homes needs to feel inspiring, not stuffy. Antique plates can be placed on stands, while art pieces create more impact when grouped together on a gallery wall. Colour palettes spark my creativity when it comes to styling new displays; I like to arrange items that blend tonally and then throw in one item in a contrasting flash of colour that makes the whole thing pop.

ARTISAN COLLECTION
A deep windowsill provides a space bathed in natural light for a collection of tactile artisan ceramics and bottle vases made from recycled glass (*this page*). Small shelf units can house a collection of smaller vessels, creating a colourful display (*opposite*).

OBJECTS OF DESIRE

Whether you're drawn to ceramic vases, stoneware pots, decorative plates or embroidered textiles, use your objects of desire to add a decorative touch to a heritage home.

WORKS OF ART
This rugged chap is landscape artist Frank Gresley, painted by Harold Gresley, and the great, great grandfather of the owner of this room. Portraits such as this look perfectly at home alongside a cluster of antique wares (*above*). This beautiful Great Vine wallpaper from the Historic Royal Palaces collection by Cole & Son in the Aqua colourway makes a fitting backdrop for a gallery wall (*opposite*).

Add Character

Make the most of high ceilings – draw attention to them with vertical displays, such as these flowers hung up to dry, or suspend a collection of baskets. Tall cupboards look great draped with hop bines.

bring comfort

Cosy soft furnishings, rugs and textiles make a home into a comfortable retreat. Cushions shouldn't be underestimated, as they have the ability to transform furniture as well as bring an inviting mood to a room. Choose ones made from textural weaves, with velvet trims and elegant ruffles. Windows can be warmed up with thick, lined curtains and fitted blinds/shades, which keep draughts at bay as well as improving acoustics. Add gentle lighting with shaded lamps or light a scented candle. Tablecloths can be used on dining tables and side tables to soften angular furniture or to add a lighter touch to brown wood pieces – I'm loving the current revival of tablecloths with frilly edging. Layering is key to comfort, so dress furniture and beds with wool blankets – look out for antique Welsh blankets, as they are having a moment right now. Finally, add warmth underfoot with natural fibre rugs and wool carpets.

COSY & INVITING

A collection of cushions made from richly textured fabrics invites you to relax in this cosy living space (*above left*). Ruched linen blinds/shades in a flamboyant Cornucopia design by Flora Soames make a snug window treatment (*above centre*). A stair runner in rich hues features a chunky weave pattern that feels warm underfoot (*above right*). This Georgian living space is layered with silk and linen textiles. The Rochester Instant Table from The Dormy House, here dressed with a fringed cloth, is a nod back to a 1980s trend; it has been in production since 1983 (*opposite*).

TEXTURAL LAYERING

A living room and bedroom, both designed by Anna Haines, feature warming colours and textural designs. The living space includes a mix of patterns that works together tonally, from the blue marble-effect lampshade by Rosi de Ruig to the cushions made from Benjelloun fabric by Bennison Fabrics, Mosul embroidered linen by Vaughan Designs and antique deep red paisley cushions sourced via Nick Jones Antiques (*this page*). Lewis & Wood's Jasper Peony wallpaper, designed by Adam Calkin, features a chinoiserie pattern and has been teamed with soft blue linen, cushions and a Welsh blanket (*opposite*).

Add Character

Wallpaper is a great way to add character to a room; bring the heritage look to a new home by choosing a historical design. In older properties, wallpaper does a good job of covering cracks too.

lighting

Get the lighting right and a room will just seem to gel. The best approach is to combine different light sources in every space, from lamps to wall lights to floor lamps. Soft lighting is more flattering and romantic, and will make a room feel more cosy in the evening or on dark winter days. I'm not a fan of harsh overhead lighting, but I do think pendants and chandeliers are essential ingredients and work well with plaster ceiling roses to bring a heritage look to any space. Anglepoise is my go-to brand for desk lights, their iconic designs being entwined with the heritage style. If you want hidden wiring on wall lights and ceiling lights, this needs to be considered before a renovation project and an electrician booked. On the same subject, if you source a vintage or antique light fitting, make sure the wiring is safe and certified before using – it's best to have the item inspected and tested by a trained electrician.

SOFTLY LIT

Pretty lighting solutions made from metal and glass can be used to add a period or modern flavour to a space. An opaque glass shade and industrial-style bracket wall light has been fitted with a vintage-look filament bulb, bringing a tailored feel to a smart kitchen (*above left*). An ornate gilded brass double wall light strikes a note of glamour in a Georgian bedroom (*above centre*). I love these delicate French fluted lampshades in milk glass, and this example looks particularly striking against deep forest green walls (*above right*).

NATURAL HUES

Elizabeth Rose's hand-painted lampshades feature thickly painted impasto brushstrokes that add texture along with colour (*above left and left*). A pop of red in the shape of angled metal over-bed lights brings a jolly touch to this twin bedroom (*above*). This sculpted rattan pendant shade gives textural interest to this attic bedroom and works well with the unusual angles (*left*).

natural flourishes

Botanical elements are the finishing touch that every room needs, from little posies of scented flowers in a vase next to a bed to a jungly collection of house plants in a humid bathroom. Adding greenery to a room brings it to life and connects you to the natural world outside. I'm a devoted fan – in fact, one of my previous books, *Botanical Style*, is all about styling your home with cut flowers, foraged branches and house plants. Fruit can also be used to add a natural flourish – when seasonally abundant, fill bowls with apples and pears for an edible and beautiful display. Source flowers direct from your garden or locally from florists who stock ethically sourced blooms and celebrate the passing months with whatever's in season.

Natural flourishes can also come in the form of collected twigs, sticks and dried seed heads arranged artfully in a statement vase. In the autumn months, I like to collect brown bracken fronds while out on country walks, which I then allow to dry out fully before displaying in oversized containers. In early spring, I bring in pots planted up with narcissi bulbs and make a display of them all along my mantelpiece. When the delicate flowers, with their delicious scent,

NATURE'S TREASURES

Branches of spring blossom add a lighter touch to this black ceramic vase and give the room a note of spring with a sweet, subtle scent (*opposite left*). You can enjoy scented pelargoniums before and after they flower, as it's the leaves that release the fresh scents (*opposite right*). A colourful vase of high-summer blooms adorns this dark marble fireplace and reminds us to stop and admire the flowers at this time of year (*above left*). Wild grasses gathered together and arranged in a tall vase create a slightly more masculine mood (*above*).

have died off, I unearth and store the bulbs until the autumn, and then plant them out in the garden for another year's display.

House plants have been popular since the Victorian era and have come and gone in and out of fashion ever since. Right now, with social media playing its part and more people seeking clean air and mindful moments, house plants are probably more popular than ever before. They are a quick fix too, as you can buy them ready grown and if placed in the right spot – one with plenty of natural light that's not too cold – they won't need that much looking after.

Heritage
SPACES

Welcoming HALLWAYS & ENTRANCES

Hallways and entrances set the scene for a home, yet so often they are a missed opportunity, becoming dead spaces filled with the clutter of coats, bikes and discarded shoes. The good news is that with few small interventions, your entrance can become something of a style statement. Even the narrowest entry can accommodate a skinny shelf, perhaps a single plank of wood on two curvaceous brackets painted the same colour as the wall, while a runner can bring colour and pattern as well as making the space look more finished. Hang a practical coat rail and a few favourite artworks, and you're done.

COME ON IN

This grand Victorian front door has been painted in a down-to-earth, grounding shade of blue, De Nimes by Farrow & Ball (*left*). The brick porch allows just enough space for a welcoming potted hydrangea. In the hallway of a different house, a large expanse of bare wall is the perfect spot for a gallery of family photos, old maps and framed wallpaper samples (*opposite*). You really can put together anything that takes your fancy, so think outside the box when creating your own display. Don't forget to include a mirror so that you can check your hair on your way out the door.

NOOKS & HOOKS
This little nook in a charming Dorset cottage is home to a collection of baskets (*above*). The panelling and cupboard have been painted in Calke Green by Farrow & Ball. The same shade connects the front door of an Arts and Crafts house to the nearby plants (*above left*). Inside, vintage hooks keep the hallway tidy (*opposite*).

cottage charm

Imagine a picture-postcard rural scene, and it is quite likely that a country cottage will spring to mind. I'm thinking about a chocolate-box pretty cottage with wild and scented rambling roses scrambling around the porch. If you want to bring some cottagecore style and a sense of nostalgia into your entrance and hallway space, consider placing pots planted with flowers by your front door – one on either side will bring a sense of formality. Climbing plants with scented flowers, such as wisteria, roses or jasmine, are a great option if you want to train a plant to cover your porch or scramble up the exterior of your home. When the flowers are in bloom, the floral scent will drift inside with you. For your hallway, search flea markets, junk shops and brocantes for antique or vintage hooks and pegboards on which to hang bags and coats. A palette of warm whites and fresh greens will always suit a cottage scheme.

BLENDED TONES

The grand entrance of this seaside townhouse in Hove, East Sussex has been expertly designed to celebrate the original stained glass, elegant staircase, Victorian tiled flooring and decorative mouldings (*this page and opposite*). The palette is refined and materials are natural. The lighting has been kept simple, from the metal wall lights with neat glass shades to the large lantern that hangs overhead.

elegant entryways

The balance between respecting the history of a property and meeting the requirements of modern-day living can be achieved with a considered palette, good design and a personal touch. This smart hallway, designed by Emma Milne, features a pared-back scheme that allows the architectural details to shine. A jute runner, which continues up the stairs, adds warmth without covering up the Victorian floor tiles. The soft amber, rich brown and delicate parchment tones of the stained-glass panels are echoed in the antique mahogany table and polished banister. The walls, woodwork/trim and ceiling are all painted in Portland Stone Deep by Little Greene. If you are having trouble choosing just one paint colour, paint large swatches on the walls and observe them at different times of the day to see which one you are most drawn to.

CLEVER CLADDING

Let the entrance to your home greet you with a comfortable bench and ample storage tucked away under the stairs (*opposite*). In this scheme by Emma Milne, the limestone flags in the hallway continue across the ground floor, making way for a natural carpet runner on the staircase (*below*). The panelling was made by Thorncombe Design & Build (*left*). If you haven't inherited original features, you can add your own detailing in the form of retro-style light fittings like the one shown below and tongue-and-groove cladding. Paint it with an eggshell finish for durability.

PAINTED DETAILS
Most halls can accommodate a single chair or a slim bench (*left*). The door and skirting boards/baseboards have been given a smart coat of paint in Railings by Farrow & Ball. In our own hallway, I have used paint to zone the space – my husband installed the tongue and groove, which we painted in a warm brown (*opposite*). The display on the marble-topped cupboard includes flowers from the garden and a tiny sculpture of *The Little Mermaid* – a souvenir from a trip to Copenhagen that evokes happy memories as I skip out the door.

keep it simple

Uncluttered, calm entrance spaces invite you in, so storage is a must for shoes, coats and keys. Keeping tidy is all about having systems in place. For instance, choosing a lovely basket to hold all your shoes will look so much nicer than leaving them in a pile by the doorway. Simple spaces benefit from a clear colour scheme, so that the eye doesn't jump around too much – choose colours you find calming. Furniture can be rustic as well as simple. I like to combine antique furniture with contemporary lighting – a trendy modern lamp can enhance an older piece of furniture and such unexpected pairings help to establish a balance between the old and the new. Styling can be both practical and visually appealing. Consider a stone bowl placed to collect the mail and keys or a chair in the perfect spot for putting shoes on. Simplicity doesn't mean your space has to be stark and impersonal, just considered.

OBJECTS OF DESIRE

The Walter table light, by heritage brand Original BTC, has a unique 1960s feel. With its striking combination of satin brass and anthracite glass, it adds a modern element to our hallway.

GROWN-UP CALM

This living space by interior designer Emma Milne manages to be at once elegant and informal, sophisticated and homely, modern and rustic. Emma's use of classic furniture, subtle yet warm colours and heavy linen curtains enhances the architectural elements of the room. Antiques and fine George Smith sofas sit happily alongside contemporary lighting and textiles in a mixture of patterns and textures (*opposite*). The giant glazed bookcase, one of many characterful period finds in this room, was chosen by Emma because it is the perfect size to fit the space (*right*).

Relaxing LIVING ROOMS

Designing, decorating and styling heritage-style living rooms involves combining the grandeur of a bygone era with the informality of modern living. I recommend starting with the walls – consider heritage paint colours, raw or natural plaster finishes or smart panelling. Next think about flooring. Sanding down and/or painting an existing wooden floor is a budget-friendly idea, which will allow you to invest in rugs. Then add some comfortable seating – a sofa, or a collection of armchairs and pouffes if the space is small. If you are renting, the sofa will be your starting point, as you can take it with you when you move.

DECORATIVE DETAILING

In Sarah Brown's living room, an antique mahogany side table has been styled with a red resin lamp from Marianna Kennedy and paintings from different eras (*left*). The original plasterwork on the ceiling has been given a fresh coat of paint to reflect the natural light (*above*). Sarah has achieved a friendly look that is modern yet traditional – ideal for a family home (*opposite*).

modern heritage

Sometimes, using antiques and traditional furnishings can give a room a stuffy, old-fashioned atmosphere, so the key to achieving the heritage-style look is to add a modern twist. Try mixing in bold modern artworks and textiles, and combining subtle tones with brighter pops of colour. Choosing clashing and complementary hues will create a lived-in atmosphere that is ideal for a family room. In her living room, interior designer Sarah Brown has used Lilac Pink, a subtle buff pink shade from Edward Bulmer Natural Paint. It is the perfect backdrop for her collection of colourful furniture and quirky accessories. If you struggle to combine different colours and patterns, it's a good idea to gather paint samples, fabric swatches and inspirational images and put them together to create a workable design concept. I tend to go by instinct, but I do find that choosing a wall colour early on in the process will help bring everything together.

OLD HOUSE NEW TRICKS
Two sofas face each other across Sarah Brown's living room. One is upholstered in a bold herringbone fabric by Claremont and the other in a green velvet by Designers Guild. The blinds/shades feature a Nicky Haslam stripe. The mix of hues and patterns suggests a playful take on a formal drawing room.

Future Heritage

Fabrics made from sustainable natural materials and woven or block printed in short runs will stand the test of time and may become highly sought-after cloths that will be treasured by future generations.

TEAK & MARBLE
Jessie and Ivo's retro palette of fawn, teak, chocolate brown and ochre works perfectly with the impressive brown marble fireplace (*left*). Jessie's charity/thrift-shop finds include a marble lamp base that she has teamed with a fluted paper shade (*above*). Classic furniture in teak, walnut and leather from the 1960s and 1970s adds to the retro heritage feel (*opposite*).

retro mood

'Everything old is new again,' as the saying goes, and this trendy space certainly echoes that sentiment. Its owners, Jessie Cutts and Ivo Vos, have taken a slow and steady approach to the renovation of their Georgian mansion terrace in Ramsgate, Kent. Most of the items in their living room are second-hand or homemade. Jessie and Ivo tend to accumulate items from various sources and then pull them together, rather than shopping for everything in one go. Their retro sideboard, found locally at an antiques shop, provides useful storage and a surface on which to display treasured objects. The comfortable sofa, which they bought second-hand, was designed by Robin Day for Habitat in the 1960s. Making new curtains for the floor-to-ceiling French windows would have required a huge amount of fabric, so instead Jessie tracked down two pairs of extra-long, extra-wide ochre velvet curtains from eBay and tailored them to fit.

Add Character

Paul West has amassed a collection of seriously smart furniture, which includes new pieces by renowned designers and vintage items from the 1960s. Investment pieces like these can travel with you from home to home.

natural living

Sustainable materials, woods, natural textiles, stoneware ceramics and antique furniture all have a place in heritage style. This living room belonging to Paul West is uncluttered and inviting, and it oozes good design, showing that interiors rich in natural elements can still be cool. This look can be achieved in properties either new or old, in the country or city. What makes it work is the tonal colour palette and chic design elements. In particular, Paul has a great eye for sourcing stylish furniture, which he softens with woollen blankets and velvet cushions. To bring a natural living style to your home, consider uncovering or laying untreated wooden floorboards, which will add warmth and texture. Choose new or vintage furniture and accessories that are built to last and have been made in harmony with the environment. House plants in terracotta pots will help to bring a sense of the outside in.

PERFECTLY NATURAL

Paul's living room is the epitome of stylish natural living (*opposite*). Old wooden stools and side tables dotted around your living space are very useful places for lamps – seen here is a beige-coloured vintage Anglepoise lamp on a slatted table that Paul sourced from an antiques dealer (*above left*). Close to the window is another lamp, which he made himself using an old stoneware pot, a DIY lamp kit and a simple shade (*above centre*). A vase filled with foraged grasses, foliage or branches establishes a link to the natural world outside (*above right*).

TAKE A MOMENT
When my husband Dave and I opened up the fireplace in our dining room and installed a log-burning stove, I decided to create this seating area using two mid-century-style chairs (*this page*). A painting by Dave of his grandparents' house hangs above the fireplace. This is a cosy spot in which to relax and drink tea. I love arranging flowers from our garden to place on the coffee table (*opposite*).

COMPACT COUNTRY

An artful mix of rustic pieces, modern shapes and heritage elements pulls this room together. Books are tucked away in a glazed cabinet and built-in shelves below the staircase, while panelling adds texture to the wall behind the sofa (*right*). A simple wooden shelf on brackets, painted the same colour as the wall, acts as a mantelpiece – an idea that's inexpensive and easy to recreate over any fireplace opening. The low milking stool and jug of orange physalis (Chinese lanterns) completes a cosy fireside scene (*opposite*).

character cottage

Heritage style is not reliant upon a home that boasts soaring ceilings and double doors. It can also bring charm and interest to smaller spaces by adopting a modest yet inviting cottage-style aesthetic. In this home, a tiny sitting room with a chunk taken out of one corner to accommodate the staircase punches above its weight thanks to its calming traditional decor with a slightly retro flavour. The room's original floorboards are painted a rich chocolate brown that manages to simultaneously ground the space while receding into the background, making it feel larger than it really is. Walls were given a coat of Farrow & Ball's Hardwick White – a subdued grey-green. To this subtle backdrop, the owner has added vibrant orange details in the shape of light fittings, a 19th-century kilim and a curvy contemporary urn. These pick up the bricks of the fire recess and add a fresh modern note to the snug interior.

COLOURFUL COTTAGECORE

There are so many charming details in Genevieve Harris's Arts and Crafts living space (*this page, opposite and overleaf*). The lead windows, wood beams and brick paver flooring are all original. Genevieve has brought her love of antiques and the English countryside together to give the room a cottagecore feel. From vases of freshly picked garden flowers to handcrafted blankets, throws and rugs, the scheme is fun and colourful, and takes inspiration from nature and from history.

Add Character

Elizabeth Rose has brought colour to this corner of her living room by painting the built-in bookcase Yellow-Pink and the window frame in Canton, both by Little Greene. These bold hues contrast with the simple plastered walls.

SIGNATURE LOOK

Joinery painted in contrasting colours is
Elizabeth Rose's signature look (*opposite*).
A hand-painted lampshade and a cushion from
her homeware collection complete her scheme.
The original fireplace has been replastered
and a neat log-burning stove installed (*left*).
Elizabeth commissioned a carpenter to build
a bookcase in the wonky alcove (*above*).

modern eclectic

Artist and designer Elizabeth Rose planned a colour scheme for each room of her Dorset
cottage. However, once the renovations were complete, she noticed how beautifully the natural
lime plaster on the walls reflected the light and decided not to cover it up with paint. Instead,
she elected to incorporate her chosen colours into the joinery. Painting window frames in
a brighter shade than the walls will add a modern feel to your room, especially if you have
windows with deep-set frames. Then you can bring in handmade pieces and different textures
for an eclectic twist. The rest of the room has a charming mix of old and new items, including
a vintage armchair reupholstered in on-trend wool bouclé. Decorative antique vases, baskets
filled with plants and a patterned fabric blind/shade set the scene. I also love the view from this
room of the local launderette/laundromat and all its comings and goings.

OBJECTS OF DESIRE

'Mantelscaping' is a key trend on social media right now. The idea is to style up a mantelpiece with objects of desire, flowers, house plants and other trinkets. Have a go yourself, then take a snap to share online.

FEMININE TOUCHES

Textural raw plaster walls have a natural clay pink tone to them, as seen in this space designed by Sophie Rowell (*this page and opposite*). Sophie painted the door and window frames in a similar shade, which she mixed herself to blend in with the walls. This subtle earthy pink shade, teamed with frilly linen fabric panels at the windows, floral paintings and ceramics, soft lighting and a bespoke striped sofa, gives the room a romantic, nostalgic feel. Raw plaster walls should be coated with a water-based polyurethane sealant to prevent them from turning yellow over time.

Entertaining
KITCHEN
& DINING
AREAS

The place where meals are made and friends and family gather, our kitchens need to be both functional and inviting. If your kitchen just needs refreshing, consider repainting your cupboards and adding smart new handles. A full redesign can be daunting and expensive, but the heritage-style look is timeless and will not date. Wooden fitted kitchens, vintage freestanding units (such as butcher's blocks) and even restaurant-style stainless-steel fittings can all fit into this aesthetic; just steer away from anything ultra modern. I especially love Shaker-style cupboards with brushed metal or polished brass hardware. An inherited, antique or artisan-made dining table is ideal for entertaining. Add a mix of chairs, benches or stools from different eras and made from a variety of materials.

FORM & FUNCTION
Here, the bank of cupboards and long table – acquired from a monastery by a Belgian antiques dealer – lead the eye to the large sash window. A tonal palette of dark blue, natural wood and Farrow & Ball's Slipper Satin highlights the decorative plasterwork. The marble worktop adds a modern heritage twist (*right*).

This Victorian kitchen/dining room designed by Paul West shows off his collection of reclaimed and vintage items. An old Ercol chair in one corner has a mustard linen cushion that brings out the warmth of the wood and the ochre tones in the mid-century Swedish painting (*left*). An Original BTC floor lamp is on hand for the evenings, while a stoneware food storage jar salvaged from the kitchen of a grand country house has been repurposed as a planter. The shelf above the kitchen sink is made from reclaimed wood (*opposite*).

reclaimed & reimagined

I always like to advocate the use of reclaimed materials as part of a sustainable approach to building and decorating. These elements have their own history – for instance, display shelves made from reclaimed wood might have grooves, stamp markings or nail marks, which will add character to your kitchen. Salvaged and vintage items are key to bringing the heritage look together, especially in a newly built property, as these finds show signs of age and patina that will ground your interiors schemes. You can source reclaimed accessories at antiques fairs, markets and junk shops, and online. During lockdown, many small antiques dealers began selling their wares via Instagram and hosting live sale events, some of which are continuing even as life returns to normal. Heritage items to look out for as you decorate your kitchen include painterly artworks, wooden chopping/cutting boards and stoneware pots and jugs/pitchers.

Future Heritage

Stoneware is having a revival, so seek out pieces you love made by hand from makers who are local to you. Or have a go at making your own pieces to display and use in the kitchen.

WOOD & STONEWARE

Two of the oldest and most sustainable materials are used in harmony in Paul West's kitchen. Paul displays his collection of stoneware ceramics on a wooden trolley (*left*). Some of the pieces are vintage, some he has made himself and others were purchased from local artisans (*above left*). Paul has created a modern kitchen with a period feel, in keeping with the age of his property (*opposite and above*). Natural materials, antique furniture, chic lighting and balanced colours have been brought together to create a timeless look.

classic good looks

Marble surfaces and a restrained palette will add an elegant feel to your kitchen. If your budget won't stretch to Italian Carrara marble, perhaps you can source a piece of reclaimed marble instead. This kitchen, designed by Emma Milne and produced by Plain English, combines subtle charcoal and navy tones with off-white and natural stone. I like the idea of the island unit being a darker hue than the wall-mounted cupboards. A classic Shaker-style kitchen perfectly fits into a heritage home and this classic look has been featured in many interiors magazines. I love to visit stylish kitchen showrooms, particularly those of brands such as Neptune and deVOL. To give your kitchen classic good looks, choose well-made and thoughtfully designed cupboards and smart brass handles, limit yourself to a few carefully chosen colours and materials and make sure you incorporate clever storage so that you can hide away clutter.

MIXED MATERIALS

An antique stoneware water jug/pitcher and handmade glass tumblers complement an old kitchen table (*above left*). A set of painted wooden shelves provides space to display glassware and cooking pots (*above centre*). A Crittall screen with ribbed glass panes divides the kitchen from a pantry space while allowing light to flood into the main kitchen area (*above right*). A classic kitchen in the basement of a Victorian townhouse in Hove, East Sussex features Plain English cupboards, a Carrara marble splashback, a blue fossil stone countertop and antique glass lights (*opposite*).

Add Character

Paint the window frames to match your kitchen cupboards, hang artworks on the walls, add cushions to furniture and, if you have space, find a nook for a stylish and comfortable safari-style armchair.

clever colour

Matching the kitchen cabinetry to the walls and woodwork/trim is a paint technique called colour drenching. The colour that interior designer Sarah Brown has committed to in her kitchen, shown here, is Silver Polish, a chalky pink from Plain English. It works so well with the hints of black, brass and natural wood from the appliances and accessories she has chosen for the rest of the space.

Colour drenching is a great technique if you are planning a makeover of an existing kitchen. Most cupboards can be repainted, but just make sure you do your research and prep the area with a good primer. Continue the colour across walls, ceilings and woodwork, ensuring you use the right paint on each surface.

This technique would look lovely in dark tones as well as lighter ones, so I am currently working on plans with my husband to redesign our kitchen with forest green cabinets. I think forgoing wall cupboards is a good idea if you have enough storage space for all the bits and pieces. A display shelf (or several) is a great way to pep up a room – just add some styling finishing touches and display accessories in contrasting colours.

SHELF DISPLAY

This lovely Plain English kitchen is painted in Silver Polish from the brand's own range. The wall cupboards have been replaced with a long shelf, and a brass rail underneath is home to everyday mugs, copper pans and enamel ladles. Sarah's collections of oil paintings and French confit pots add personality to the space (*right*).

DECORATIVE JOINERY

Carpentry plays a major role in heritage kitchens and dining spaces. Interior designer Sarah Brown has created an informal eating area in her kitchen, which includes a custom-built bench made by Plain English and a farmhouse-style table with a base that's been painted in the same shade of burgundy (*opposite*). Sarah's kitchen leads into a more formal dining room, which is bathed in natural light (*left*). This space features a custom-built corner cupboard that was designed to fit an existing alcove and painted in a sunny yellow tone (*above and above left*).

Future Heritage

Many well-crafted items have the potential to become future heritage pieces. In this Georgian home, a cast-iron and brass wall light by Tom Dixon casts light through the internal glazing into a Shaker-style kitchen (opposite).

FAMILY RECIPE

As you enter this kitchen, you become aware of
the original stone flooring, which is well trodden
and worn in places (*below and opposite*). It reveals
the age of the building, dating back to the 15th
century. An oval table sits in the centre of the
room. Placing the furniture this way has made the
space the hub of family life; on cooler days these
are the best seats in the house, as they are close
to the Aga range cooker. The table is often laden
with delicious bakes, such as this chocolate cake
decorated with garden roses (*right*).

vintage style

Yellow is becoming a go-to colour for those seeking
to add a cheerful feel-good factor to an interior. Here,
Genevieve Harris has painted her kitchen cupboards
in Haymarket by Mylands Paint. Her Arts and Crafts
house is full of quirky touches and the pop of yellow
suits her vintage style. If vibrant yellow feels too bright
for you, steer towards muted mustard, ochre and
turmeric tones for a burst of golden sunshine.

Genevieve is a keen baker and home cook, and her
welcoming kitchen is where she bakes delicious cakes
using handed-down family recipes, such as the divine
chocolate cake pictured above. The kitchen/dining
room is furnished with an array of rustic pieces, mostly
collected from car boot/yard sales and vintage fairs.
Her antique Windsor armchair, positioned by the
range cooker with a plump vintage red floral print
cushion on the seat, invites you to sit and relax.

SETTING THE MOOD

Jessie Cutts and Ivo Vos have preserved the original features in the dining room of their seafront home in Kent, which is used for home schooling and informal gatherings (*opposite*). The hemp rug, gingham tablecloth and assorted chairs have a homely feel. One of Jessie's quilted cushions softens a rattan chair (*this page*).

eclectic salvage

This is such a fun space, but it has also been built for serious cooking and features all the mod cons any home chef could wish for, as well as an Aga range cooker. Designed by homeowner Bella Middleton, it is filled with out-of-the-ordinary touches and fantastic display ideas. Bella has made the most of the large, open apex ceiling to display her eclectic installations. Her modern stainless-steel kitchen cupboard and island units perfectly blend with her antique wood cupboard filled with collected family glass and ceramics. The dining space has been created with cosy suppers with her friends and family in mind. The room benefits from overhead task lights as well as low-level lamps, with shades that soften harsh light in the evenings. To create a similar vibe in your kitchen, try using the ceiling space for an impromptu display and put house plants in vintage ceramic pots or large bowls.

COLLECTED & CURATED

Bella Middleton's kitchen is peppered with warm tones, from antique woods to natural basket weaves. The space could have felt cluttered, but keeping the walls fresh and white makes it feel more like a gallery space. The paintings in the dining area add interest to a spare wall (*opposite*). The art doesn't have to be expensive – you can frame children's drawings, buy paintings from local art fairs or even have a go at creating your own pieces. In the main kitchen area, earthy red curtains screen off the pantry and the door to the hallway (*below*).

PRETTY DREAMS

Raw plaster walls provide a muted clay pink backdrop for the bedroom of Jessie Cutts and and Ivo Vos, who chose a matching paint colour for the woodwork/trim (*opposite*). Their smart Teramo bed by Ercol is dressed with cotton ticking bed linen, luxe velvet cushions in burnt orange and a quilt designed and handmade by Jessie. Its geometric pattern adds a modern edge. In this bathroom, dual sink vanity units and a roll-top tub with claw feet are both pretty and practical (*right*). With soft pink walls in Cuisse de Nymphe Emue by Edward Bulmer Natural Paint, it is a relaxing place to be.

Soothing
BEDROOMS &
BATHROOMS

When designing and decorating a space for sleeping, it is vital to make it a calming environment that will promote a good night's sleep. Start with a soothing palette of subtle, muted tones and minimal patterns. Textures will also help to create an inviting atmosphere, so choose breathable cotton or linen bedding and warming wools and velvets for cushions and throws. A similar approach can be just as effective in our bathrooms: paint the walls in tonal hues and choose neutral accessories such as baskets, hemp rugs and vintage glass jars for storage.

Future Heritage

Elizabeth Rose's hand-painted shades for wall lights and table lamps have a timeless appeal. Along with her embroidered Tulips cushion, these designs will be cherished by future generations.

patina of the past

In the main bedroom of her Dorset cottage, designer Elizabeth Rose has exposed the original beams, which provide a rustic patina and complement the distinctive original doorway. The extra door behind the bed was discovered during her renovation – it can't be accessed from the other side, but Elizabeth has kept it as a feature, preferring not to cover it up again when she replastered the walls. The room is simply furnished with a comfortable bed, a lamp table and a rattan peacock chair. The whole scheme is brought together by Elizabeth's personal touches, which include her framed family heirloom hand-painted tile from the Coalport China Company and her own cushion designs and hand-painted lampshades. The authentic Indian kantha throw and the fireplace painted in Little Greene's Tuscan Red paint add colour to the scheme.

ADDED COLOUR

Elizabeth Rose has dressed her bed with crisp white cotton bedding, a kantha throw and a painterly Tulips cushion from her homeware collection (*below*). She has added colour to the room by painting the fireplace red (*opposite left*). In a space next to the chimneybreast, Elizabeth has placed a vintage rattan peacock chair and added another cushion from her range.

WORK IN PROGRESS

The heritage style isn't all about polished rooms and completed renovation projects, so relax and enjoy the process. A recent DIY project for Jessie Cutts and Ivo Vos involved removing layers of paint from this internal door in their Georgian house, which they are now reluctant to cover up again (*this page*). They have also stripped the peeling yellow wallpaper in their bathroom (*opposite*). The bare plaster adds charm and suits the age of the property. Jessie has sewn a fabric skirt to conceal the storage below the sink – this would be a great quick fix if you are renting.

Carefully chosen accessories pull together this modern-meets-period scheme. Paul's use of colour is clear and considered, and he shows a preference for natural materials such as woods, linens, marble, stone, paper, glass and wool. Heritage elements include a vintage Welsh blanket woven with beige and fawn threads into a traditional pattern (*below*), and an Original BTC Hector table light, which is set to be a future heritage piece (*left*). The large bay window's original shutters have been carefully restored and even the black metal Victorian-style radiator was chosen to fit the scheme (*opposite*).

contemporary design & muted colours

One of the key ingredients when decorating a soothing bedroom space is a muted colour palette. This is expertly demonstrated here by designer Paul West, who has created a relaxing, calm basement bedroom in a busy part of London. Paul designed the modern four-poster bed himself and hired a carpenter to build it. He also sanded the original floorboards and added a natural woven rug for comfort. The large bay window is another stunning original feature and the shutters help to diffuse the light on sunny days. The room has been painted in two shades of white by Farrow & Ball and is styled with understated pieces that allow the architecture to shine. Crisp white bedding and an oversized rice-paper globe shade from Hay are offset by the rustic French confit pot, demonstrating how old and new can work together.

EASY ELEGANCE

When muted tones are used to
decorate and style a space with
period characteristics, the results
can take on an easy elegance. Linen
curtains in a bathroom establish a
grown-up mood while adding much-
needed softness (*this page*). In the
same house, a smart bedroom
features a surprising amount of
texture, from the pleated silk
lampshade on the wall light to the
headboard covered in a soft grey
ticking stripe (*opposite*). The cushions
are made from a mix of linens and
soft wool, and the foot of the bed
is covered with a quilted throw.

WASHED LINEN

Simple white wall tiles and smart black fixtures and fittings give Paul West's bathroom a smart, contemporary look (*this page and opposite*). To add a heritage element, he has repurposed an antique wooden cupboard and added a Belfast sink to make a vanity unit. A natural linen shower curtain with waterproof lining tones with his wood-framed mirror and stool. Take notice of the two-tone painted wall – the upper half has a matt surface while the lower half, which is more prone to being splashed, has a durable gloss finish that adds a practical design element.

SLEEP & SOAK
Bringing vintage elements into a bathroom can soften an all-white bathroom suite (*above*). Old side tables and small cabinets will help keep clutter to a minimum. Try sewing your own shower curtain with a waterproof lining and lace ruffles. A light and airy bedroom is the perfect setting for a bedspread in a beautiful vintage floral fabric (*above left and opposite*).

soft vintage

The home of interior-design consultant Sophie Rowell is a lesson in how to incorporate antique finds into a fresh new look. She has opened up the bedroom ceiling to the rafters, which she has painted white along with the walls to bring a light and airy feel to the space. Window treatments have been kept minimal to make the most of the sea views. She sources vintage items for her home and design projects from fairs, junk shops and flea markets. The white walls of the bedroom are the perfect backdrop for some of these items, from wonky wooden stools to giant stone urns. The bed has a plush headboard upholstered in a soft ticking fabric and is dressed with layered linens. A floral bedspread adds to the romantic aesthetic. If you, too, are a fan of vintage items, consider painting your space in pale colours to help your favourite items stand out. Cushions and other textiles in faded vintage florals will add a feminine touch.

Add Character

If you mix and clash vintage patterns in a room, it stops the overall look becoming twee. Deciding which textiles might work together is a matter of trial and error until you find a combination that works for you.

imperfect women

heritage styling

My husband renovated our spare bedroom during the initial weeks of the first UK lockdown due to the Covid-19 pandemic. This space has views across our garden, so we decided to move our main bedroom from the front of the house to here. We wanted the room to have a modern heritage feel with decorative joinery, classic colours and heritage materials, so Dave got to work rebuilding some of the walls and then installing the panelling, which we ordered from The English Panelling Company. We painted this in Farrow & Ball's Railings, while the rest of the room is School House White, including the metal fire surround, which is a more recent addition. Our bespoke bed from The Dormy House has a deep buttoned headboard upholstered in luxe linen and a Silentnight mattress made from eco-friendly materials. It is important to me when sourcing new items that they are not made using plastics, unless they are recycled. I've dressed the bed with lovely linen bedding and gingham and embroidered cushions.

GARDEN VIEWS

An oil painting by my late grandfather, Ronald Lake, takes pride of place on our new little mantelpiece (*above*). Dave fitted our Anglepoise Original 1227 wall lights on either side of our new bed (*opposite above left*). My cushions are from Projektityyny (*opposite above centre*). A cup of tea is especially reviving while enjoying the garden views from this armchair (*opposite above right and below*).

Add Character

Attention to detail is a sure-fire way to add character to a room. I am especially fond of brass fixtures and fittings, so we matched our black and brass wall lights to our brass light switches and door handles.

CURTAIN CALL

Window treatments can sometimes be an afterthought and are often expensive, especially if they need to be made to measure. However, a well-made set of curtains in fabrics that work with the rest of the scheme can add luxury detail to a space. For ages after we moved to this house we had budget-friendly unlined cotton panels at the windows, but as we decorate each room we are investing in tailor-made curtains in linens and velvets (*left*). They have really changed the feel of the rooms.

BATHROOM GOALS

My husband and I designed our bathroom with the aim of bringing hotel luxury to our Victorian house. We inherited this pretty chandelier from Dave's Nanna Peggy (*above*). The sink unit was a set of tired but well-made drawers that we found in a junk shop (*left*). Dave reveneered the drawers, added a marble top and brass knobs and fitted a new sink and taps/faucets. Victorian-inspired floor tiles from Fired Earth introduce a subtle pattern (*above left*). Dave lined the walls with white metro tiles and fitted a new tub and shower, then painted the doorway to complete the space (*opposite*).

a bold approach

I don't believe that stripes ever truly go out of fashion, but right now they seem to be everywhere and picking up pace as a design staple. If a restrained, muted scheme is not your thing, consider bringing a bolder design idea to your bedroom and bathroom with stripes. This impressive wall pattern created by the artist Russell Loughlan has been painstakingly achieved with patience, a steady hand and a few rolls of masking tape. Note the change of tone in the opposite wall and the shadow effect in the section directly under the picture rail, which I think slightly softens the look and makes it more appropriate for a bedroom. If you don't have the time or inclination to paint the stripes yourself, simply choose a wallpaper with a similar design. In a room with plain walls, stripes can be incorporated via the bed linen. Wide stripes will have more of an impact than skinny ones, so bear that in mind if you want a bold, eye-catching effect.

FULL-ON STRIPES
Russell has introduced red accents with his original artwork and a quilt from Will & Yates in Deal, Kent (*opposite*). Across the room, stripes in a lighter shade are echoed in the grooves on the cabinet doors (*below left*). Verdigris Green by Farrow & Ball has been used to continue the stripes into the bathroom (*below*).

PRACTICAL SPACES

Home offices, studios, boot rooms & pantries

Every home requires at least one practical space – it can be as simple as a set of coat hooks or an entire room for working from home. During the Covid-19 pandemic, our need for practical spaces doubled as our homes became our schools, offices, creative spaces and restaurants. In smaller homes, where a spare-room takeover is not an option, practical spaces need to be carved out wherever possible, so think creatively. Could you incorporate a pantry into your kitchen? A desk in a hallway can become a home office, while a cupboard can be fitted with peg rails and a built-in bench to make a miniature boot room.

AVAILABLE SPACE
In this stylish two-floor London apartment in a converted Victorian townhouse, a space to work has been made at the top of the stairs (*left*). It is a great spot with a lovely view over the garden, which can be accessed via a set of steps beyond the glass door. The teak antique desk is teamed with a rush-seated mid-century chair. An Anglepoise desk lamp provides task lighting. The attic of a Georgian seaside house serves as a studio for its artist owner (*opposite*). Decorative plates, photographs and artworks hang on the wall. The monochrome decor keeps the space feeling uncluttered.

working from home

The pandemic has resulted in more people working at home than ever before, with guest bedrooms, dining-room tables and living spaces having to become multi-use. We have also had to think about our backdrops for online meetings, so existing home offices may be in need of smartening up. Bringing heritage style to your workspace can be done by choosing furniture that either has a history to it or has been made to last by a skilled craftsperson. The desk needs to be a table at the right height for you to sit at comfortably. You will also need a chair that can properly support you all day long. However, just because it is an office, that doesn't mean you have to choose function over style. A space with natural light is the best option, as it will encourage greater productivity, and using house plants to decorate it will ensure the air is rich in oxygen. I prefer working in a calm space, in which the walls are painted in soft, pale and natural tones from a heritage collection. I also prefer not to be surrounded by clutter. This is not always my reality, but good storage is a must. Finally, a few well-chosen trinkets, scented candles or framed photographs can evoke fond memories and give your mind a break.

OBJECTS OF DESIRE

Since the 1930s, Anglepoise has been producing its iconic desk lamps. I saw new and vintage examples in nearly all the homes we visited for this book. I also have my own ever-growing collection.

NEAT, TIDY & STYLISH

In order to keep work separate from your home life, it is a good idea to keep your working space tidy and introduce storage ideas to keep it clutter free – though of course this is easier said than done. Investing in storage boxes will help you stay organized (*right*). Here, designer Paul West has created an office space along one wall of the guest bedroom in his London home (*opposite*). The desk is made from an oak plank on two trestles. The mid-century pieces have a sophisticated appeal, while the wooden surfaces and garden views feel calming and natural.

Future Heritage

Artisan quilts made from fabrics that have their own history, whether salvaged or sentimental, are sure to be treasured. Items created by skilled craftspeople will stand the test of time.

This delicate yet earthy pink is a modern take on the idea of clay- and earth-toned pigments. In this colour-drenched scheme, it highlights the architectural features of the space, such as the high skirting boards/baseboards and the wide Georgian doorway (*above left*). It also creates a backdrop for Jess's quilt samples (*opposite and above*). All the furniture and even her sewing machine is antique.

creative studio space

Jessie Cutts makes beautiful slow-stitched quilts and wall hangings via her business, Cutts & Sons, and her sewing room is the hub of her creativity. The room adjoins the living room of her home in a Georgian mansion terrace. It has large proportions and benefits from views of the Kent coastline. However, Jessie's clever use of colour stops it becoming too lofty and empty. In particular, she has used the colour-drenching paint technique to give the space an uncluttered backdrop. Colour drenching involves choosing one hue for all the different surfaces in a room, from walls and ceilings to skirting boards/baseboards and doorways. It can be achieved with the same colour in different paint finishes or varying tones. Here, Jessie has chosen Rose Tinted White by Edward Bulmer Natural Paint. The warm shade complements the natural wood flooring and creates a comfortable feel for this busy creative space.

perfect pantries & useful utility rooms

The word 'pantry' comes from the Old French word 'paneterie' and ultimately derives from 'panis', the Latin word for bread. In medieval times, bread was stored in the pantry while meat was kept in a larder. Nowadays, a pantry can either be integrated into the kitchen units, freestanding or occupy a room of its own. It is a great place in which to experiment with joyful colours and patterns. You could even install shelves in your kitchen or hallway and paint them a cheerful colour to establish a pantry area. Choose Shaker-style wood planks with decorative brackets or repurpose a dresser/hutch or bookcase. Pantries and utility rooms need good lighting, but this can still be in the heritage style – just add pendant or wall lights with fluted or opaque glass shades and filament bulbs. Keep small items in vintage tins, decant dry goods into glazed stoneware vessels and reuse glass jars for homemade pickles and preserves.

DESIGNER CARPENTRY
Bella Middleton's utility room holds bottles of organic cleaning products from her Norfolk Natural Living range. She added hooks to her storage cupboard to hang brushes and dusters (*above*). This service area designed by Emma Milne features panelling, Shaker-style shelving and cabinets by kitchen specialist Plain English (*opposite*). It is a stylish and practical choice.

STYLISH STORAGE

The dresser/hutch in Genevieve Harris's larder is stocked with homemade elderflower pressé, chutneys and preserves (*above*). Wire baskets hang from the ceiling, ready for the next harvest from her garden (*above right*). Her collection of antique glazed terracotta jars and enamel tins are used to store dry ingredients (*right*). Sarah Brown worked with Plain English to design this walk-in pantry for her London house (*opposite*). The paint colours, Chop and Nicotine, are exclusive to the brand. The delicate French glass fluted pendant light is a pretty detail.

OLD & NEW

Our outdoor lounge is our haven from spring to autumn (*opposite*). The modern rattan sofa set has a heritage vibe thanks to a mix of cushions in gingham, plain linens and soft velvets. The little oak table was commissioned from an artisan maker. On our deck, a vintage trestle table from Lamb & Newt is surrounded by an ever-changing display of pots (*right*). Introducing older pieces into a new garden will make it feel established. In a mature garden, a few antique stone planters or metal folding chairs will blend in with their surroundings as though they have always been there.

Inviting OUTSIDE SPACES

The heritage style is not exclusive to interiors – our outside spaces can also benefit from some thoughtful styling ideas that celebrate the history of gardens and are compatible with modern living. Creating a relaxing outdoor space with the heritage style is easy, as it is a look that doesn't date. Use timeworn vintage furniture and gardenalia, especially pieces that have lived their lives outdoors, as their patina and charm will bring character to a botanical setting. Well-placed seating and tables in dappled shade are sure to make your space feel comfortable and inviting.

heritage garden

This look mixes rustic elements, classic materials and artisan-made pieces with romantic touches. I suspend white cotton bunting under our apple tree as soon as the weather changes from winter to spring, as it is a wonderful time to celebrate being outside. Bluebells fill the miniature meadow next to our table, making way for wildflowers by midsummer. Towards the end of the season these are replaced by tall, feathery native grasses. This little patch has a whimsical, secret-garden feel. Throughout our outside space, which is split into different zones, I like to style with antique pieces as well as modern items. Bistro folding chairs are easy to move around – I have several vintage examples, and a couple of new ones with sturdier seats. Heavier items, such as a pair of inherited stone planters, tend to find a spot and stay put. If we do require new furniture, we try to source well-made items crafted from sustainable materials.

INTRIGUING ELEMENTS
I love to add interesting features to the different sections of our garden so that there are surprises around every corner. A concrete urn planter, which I painted black when I bought it from a junk shop, has weathered well on the rusty table under our apple tree (*above left*). The dining table is styled with linens from Projektityyny and late-summer echinacea, salvia and rudbeckia in vases, one of which is a jug from my parents' Poole Pottery wedding china set (*above centre and opposite*). A sundial inherited from my husband's grandparents has great sentimental value (*above right*).

Add Character

This rustic metal trolley was a lucky find and now provides characterful storage for pots, crates and other gardenalia. The flat top presents an opportunity to style up a pretty display of plants and decorative items.

COUNTRY CHARM

A brick-paved patio is a perfect spot for a table and chairs in this country garden (*opposite*). Raised beds fashioned from railway sleepers/railroad ties are planted with fruits, vegetables and flowers. On the table, an old dairy bowl makes an unusual vase. I have a rusty trolley on the patio in the middle of our garden (*above*). The numbered buckets were once used at flower shows and now make great pots for young plants. This tiny vintage watering can was perhaps made for children (*right*).

GARDENALIA ON PARADE

My shed is situated at the bottom of our garden; it is a little hidden gem that cannot be seen from the house. Inside, I have a wall-mounted shelf with compartments in which I showcase some of my gardenalia, such as terracotta pots, jute string and heritage gardening books (*above left*). The display also incorporates my handwoven palm leaf tray and sun hat (*opposite*). I like to use metal trays to make little outdoor vignettes – seen here is an assortment of glass bottles (*above*). I originally used these vintage metal flower buckets at the RHS Chelsea Flower Show (*left*).

TAKE A MOMENT
Set over two floors of a converted four-storey townhouse, this London apartment benefits from a private garden, accessed via patio doors at ground level and a set of exterior stairs from a doorway on the upper floor (*opposite and left*). A pair of weathered wood and metal bistro chairs and a round vintage table utilize the space by the sunny front doorway (*above*).

small suntraps

One way to extend your heritage home into the garden is to install a decked terrace. One that can be accessed from double doors is always lovely and means you can steal a quick moment in the sun when the weather is fine. It doesn't take a large space to catch some rays – even a table and chair set right outside a sunny front door can be very inviting. Town gardens look smart and chic decorated with a minimal colour palette. Charcoal black may not be an obvious choice for garden chairs, but it will give a contemporary feel to an established garden and stand out against the greenery. If you are planning a suntrap in your garden, consider zoning the space using wooden decking or stone pavers. A backdrop of beautiful old bricks is always appealing, or if your walls are rendered, consider painting them white to reflect the light.

cottage style

I am a huge fan of cottage-style gardens. This look is characterized by an informal jumble of blowsy blooms in a romantic setting. Think of a country cottage with a garden spilling over with rambling roses, spires of foxgloves and a relaxed tapestry of other colourful flowers. Cottagecore is a positive concept that embraces nostalgia for the traditional rural lifestyle; it encourages us to work in harmony with nature, for example by growing our own food and flowers. A key theme is biodiversity, which is great for our bees and other pollinators as well as for our own well-being. Aesthetically, cottagecore takes its inspiration from the English countryside. This style works well in all types of gardens, especially if you combine cottage-style planting with weathered stone, metal furniture or garden antiques. Wearing a straw hat or a floral outfit will give the job of deadheading an added charm. In established gardens with flower borders, I recommend taking a relaxed approach and letting plants self-seed naturally. A water feature is a great way to support wildlife, but consider using a characterful salvaged container rather than a new plastic tub.

FLEA-MARKET FINDS
Head to salvage, vintage and antique fairs to source your cottage-garden accessories, always considering how items can be repurposed. Here, two urn planters and a stone slab have been fashioned into a bench (*below*). This turquoise bistro table and matching chairs are not antique but definitely second-hand (*opposite*). They add a vibrant pop of colour against the wall, which is made from stone containing ammonite fossils.

Future Heritage

To plant a garden is to plan for the future. I'm so grateful to the previous owners of our garden, who planted magnolia, wisteria and an apple tree. Our choices today will have an impact on future generations.

PICTURE CREDITS

Endpapers: Interior design by Emma Milne Interiors, design and build by Thorncombe Design & Build; 1–3 The home of designers Jessie Cutts and Ivo Vos in Kent, cuttandsons.com; 4 left Sophie Rowell, interior consultant @côtedefolk, cotedefolk.com; 4 centre The Dorset home of Libby Rose of @atelierelizabethrose; 4 right The home of interior designer Sarah Brown in London, sarahbrowninteriors.com; 5 left The home of interior designer Anna Haines, annahaines.com; 5 centre The Dorset home of Libby Rose of @atelierelizabethrose; 5 right The home of designers Jessie Cutts and Ivo Vos in Kent; 6–7 The home of interior designer Sarah Brown in London, sarahbrowninteriors.com; 8 left The Dorset home of Libby Rose of atelierelizabethrose; 8 right The home of artist/interiors consultant Russell Loughlan; 9 The home of interior designer Sarah Brown in London, sarahbrowninteriors.com; 10 and 11 above The home of Bella and Hugo Middleton, norfolknaturalliving.com; 11 below and 12 The home of Genevieve Harris in Kent; 13 above left The home of interior designer Anna Haines, annahaines.com; 13 above right The home of designers Jessie Cutts and Ivo Vos in Kent, cuttandsons.com; 13 below The Dorset home of Libby Rose of @atelierelizabethrose; 14–15 The home of designers Jessie Cutts and Ivo Vos in Kent, cuttandsons.com; 16–17 Interior design by Emma Milne Interiors, design and build by Thorncombe Design & Build; 18 left Interior design by Emma Milne Interiors, design and build by Thorncombe Design & Build; 18 right The home of designers Jessie Cutts and Ivo Vos in Kent, cuttandsons.com; 19 Interior design by Emma Milne Interiors, design and build by Thorncombe Design & Build; 20 left The home of designersJessie Cutts and Ivo Vos in Kent, cuttandsons.com; 20 right and 21 The Dorset home of Libby Rose of @atelierelizabethrose; 22 left The home of interior designer Sarah Brown in London, sarahbrowninteriors.com; 22 above right The home of Bella and Hugo Middleton www.norfolknaturalliving.com; 22 below right The Dorset home of Libby Rose of @atelierelizabethrose; 23 The home of designers Jessie Cutts and Ivo Vos in Kent, cuttandsons.com; 24 styled by Selina Lake; 25 left The home of artist/interiors consultant Russell Loughlan; 25 right Sophie Rowell, interior consultant @côtedefolk, cotedefolk.com; 26 left The home of artist/interiors consultant Russell Loughlan; 26 right The home of interior designer Sarah Brown in London, sarahbrowninteriors.com; 27 The home of artist/interiors consultant Russell Loughlan; 28 left The home of Bella and Hugo Middleton, www.norfolknaturalliving.com; 28 right Interior design by Emma Milne Interiors and design and build by Thorncombe Design & Build; 29 left the Dorset home of Libby Rose of @atelierelizabethrose; 29 right The home of Bella and Hugo Middleton, norfolknaturalliving.com; 30 above left The home of designers Jessie Cutts and Ivo Vos in Kent, cuttandsons.com; 30 below left The home of interior designer Anna Haines, annahaines.com; 30 right The home of interior designer Sarah Brown in London, sarahbrowninteriors.com; 31 The family home of Bella and Hugo Middleton, norfolknaturalliving.com; 32 The home of interior designer Sarah Brown in London, sarahbrowninteriors.com; 33 Styled by Selina Lake; 34 above left The home of interior designer Sarah Brown in London, sarahbrowninteriors.com; 34 below left Styled by Selina Lake; 34 below right The Dorset home of Libby Rose of @atelierelizabethrose; 35 The Dorset home of Libby Rose of @atelierelizabethrose; 36 The home of Genevieve Harris in Kent; 37 Styled by Selina Lake; 38 The home of artist/interiors consultant Russell Loughlan; 39 left Sophie Rowell, interior consultant @côtedefolk, cotedefolk.com; 39 above and below right The home of interior designer Sarah Brown in London, sarahbrowninteriors.com; 40 The home of Bella and Hugo Middleton, norfolknaturalliving.com; 41 styled by Selina Lake; 42–43 Sophie Rowell, interior consultant @côtedefolk, cotedefolk.com; 44 left The home of artist/interiors consultant Russell Loughlan; 44 right Paul West @consideredthings; 45 The home of Bella and Hugo Middleton, norfolknaturalliving.com; 46–47 The home of interior designer Anna Haines, annahaines.com; 48 The home of interior designer Sarah Brown in London, sarahbrowninteriors.com; 49 The home of designers Jessie Cutts and Ivo Vos in Kent, cuttandsons.com; 50 The home of interior designer Anna Haines, annahaines.com; 51 Sophie Rowell, interior consultant @côtedefolk, cotedefolk.com; 52 left and 53 The home of Genevieve Harris in Kent; 52 right The home of designers Jessie Cutts and Ivo Vos in Kent, cuttandsons.com; 54 left and above right Sophie Rowell, interior consultant @côtedefolk, cotedefolk.com; 54 below right The home of Genevieve Harris in Kent; 55 Paul West @consideredthings; 56 left styled by Selina Lake; 56 right Sophie Rowell, interior consultant @côtedefolk, cotedefolk.com; 57 left The home of interior designer Anna Haines, annahaines.com; 57 right Paul West @consideredthings; 58 Sophie Rowell, interior consultant @côtedefolk, cotedefolk.com; 59 The home of interior designer Anna Haines, annahaines.com; 60 The home of Genevieve Harris in Kent; 61–63 The home of Bella and Hugo Middleton, norfolknaturalliving.com; 64 left and right The home of interior designer Anna Haines, annahaines.com; 64 centre The home of interior designer Sarah Brown in London, sarahbrowninteriors.com; 65 The home of Bella and Hugo Middleton, norfolknaturalliving.com; 66–67 The home of interior designer Anna Haines, annahaines.com; 68 left Interior design by Emma Milne Interiors and design and build by Thorncombe Design & Build; 68 centre The home of Bella and Hugo Middleton, norfolknaturalliving.com; 68 right The home of designers Jessie Cutts and Ivo Vos in Kent, cuttandsons.com; 69 above left and below the Dorset home of Libby Rose of @atelierelizabethrose; 69 above right Sophie Rowell, interior consultant @côtedefolk, cotedefolk.com; 70 left Interior design by Emma Milne Interiors, design and build by Thorncombe Design & Build; 70 right Sophie Rowell, interior consultant @côtedefolk, cotedefolk.com; 71 left The home of interior designer Anna Haines, annahaines.com; 71 right The home of artist/interiors consultant Russell Loughlan; 72–73 Sophie Rowell, interior consultant @côtedefolk, cotedefolk.com; 74 The home of interior designer Sarah Brown in London, sarahbrowninteriors.com; 75 The home of designers Jessie Cutts and Ivo Vos in Kent, cuttandsons.com; 76 and 77 left The home of Genevieve Harris in Kent; 77 right The Dorset home of Libby Rose of @atelierelizabethrose; 78–81 Interior design by Emma Milne Interiors, design and build by Thorncombe Design & Build; 81 below left The home of interior designer Anna Haines, annahaines.com; 82 Paul West @consideredthings; 83 styled by Selina Lake; 84–85 Interior design by Emma Milne Interiors, design and build by Thorncombe Design & Build; 86–89 The home of interior designer Sarah Brown in London, sarahbrowninteriors.com; 90–91 The home of designers Jessie Cutts and Ivo Vos in Kent, cuttandsons.com; 92 and 93 left and centre Paul West @consideredthings; 93 right Interior design by Emma Milne Interiors, design and build by Thorncombe Design & Build; 94–95 styled by Selina Lake; 96–97 The home of artist/interiors consultant Russell Loughlan; 98–101 The home of Genevieve Harris in Kent; 102–103 The Dorset home of Libby Rose of @atelierelizabethrose; 104–105 Sophie Rowell, interior consultant @côtedefolk, cotedefolk.com; 106–111 Paul West @consideredthings; 112–113 Interior design by Emma Milne Interiors, design and build by Thorncombe Design & Build; 114–115 The home of interior designer Anna Haines, annahaines.com; 116–119 The home of interior designer Sarah Brown in London, sarahbrowninteriors.com; 120–121 The home of artist/interiors consultant Russell Loughlan; 122–123 The home of Genevieve Harris in Kent; 124–125 The home of designers Jessie Cutts and Ivo Vos in Kent, cuttandsons.com; 126–127 The home of Bella and Hugo Middleton, norfolknaturalliving.com; 128 The home of designers Jessie Cutts and Ivo Vos in Kent, cuttandsons.com; 129 The home of interior designer Anna Haines www.annahaines.com; 130–131 The Dorset home of Libby Rose of @atelierelizabethrose; 132–133 The home of designers Jessie Cutts and Ivo Vos in Kent, cuttandsons.com; 134–135 Paul West @consideredthings; 136–137 Interior design by Emma Milne Interiors, design and build by Thorncombe Design & Build; 138–139 Paul West @consideredthings; 140–141 Sophie Rowell, interior consultant @côtedefolk, cotedefolk. com; 142–145 Styled by Selina Lake; 146–147 The home of artist/interiors consultant Russell Loughlan; 148 Paul West @ consid008things; 149 The home of artist/interiors consultant Russell Loughlan; 150–151 Paul West @consideredthings; 152–153 The home of designers Jessie Cutts and Ivo Vos in Kent, cuttandsons.com; 154 The home of Bella and Hugo Middleton, norfolknaturalliving.com; 155 Interior design by Emma Milne Interiors, design and build by Thorncombe Design & Build; 156 The home of Genevieve Harris in Kent; 157 The home of interior designer Sarah Brown in London, sarahbrowninteriors.com; 158–161 Styled by Selina Lake; 162 and 163 right The home of Genevieve Harris in Kent; 163 left styled by Selina Lake; 164–165 styled by Selina Lake; 166 and 167 left Paul West @consideredthings; 167 right Sophie Rowell, interior consultant @côtedefolk, cotedefolk.com; 168 The home of Genevieve Harris in Kent; 169 The Dorset home of Libby Rose of @atelierelizabethrose; 170–171 The home of Genevieve Harris in Kent.

BUSINESS CREDITS

Selina Lake
Author and stylist
www.selinalake.co.uk
Pages 24; 33; 34 bl; 37; 41; 56 l; 83; 94–95; 142–143; 144–145; 158–159; 160–161; 163 l; 164–165.

Atelier Elizabeth Rose
E: info@atelierelizabethrose.com
www.atelierelizabethrose.com
Pages 4 c; 5 c; 8 l; 13 b; 20 r; 21; 22 br; 29 l; 34 br; 35; 69 al; 69 bl; 77 r; 102–103; 130–131; 169.

Sarah Brown
www.sarahbrowninteriors.com
Pages 4 r; 6–7; 9; 22 l; 26 r; 30 r; 32; 34 al; 39 ar; 39 br; 48; 64 c; 74; 86–89; 116–117; 118–119; 157.

Jessie Cutts and Ivo Vos
www.cuttandsons.com
Pages 1–3; 5 r; 13 ar; 14–15; 18 r; 20 l; 23; 30 al; 49; 52 r; 68 r; 75; 90–912; 124–125; 128; 132–133; 152–153.

Anna Haines Design Ltd.
www.annahaines.com
Pages 5 l; 13 al; 30 bl; 46–47; 50; 57 l; 59; 64 l; 64 r; 66–67; 71 l; 81 bl; 114–115; 129.

Genevieve Harris
@mrs_trufflepig
Pages 11 b; 12; 36; 52 l; 53; 54 b; 60; 76; 77 l; 122–123; 156; 162; 163 r; 168; 170–171.

Russell Loughlan
@russellloghlan
@thehouseondolphinstreet
Pages 8 r; 25 l; 26 l; 27; 38; 44 l; 71 r; 96–97; 98–99; 100–101; 120–121; 146–147; 149.

Emma Milne Interiors
www.emmamilne.co.uk
and
Thorncombe Design & Build
www.thorncombe.co.uk
Endpapers; 16–17; 18 l; 19; 28 r; 68 l; 70 l; 78–81; 84–85; 93 r; 112–113; 136–137; 155.

Norfolk Natural Living
Workshop 40
East Coast Business Park
Kings Lynn
Cambridgeshire PE34 3LW
T: 01553 775758
E: hello@norfolknaturalliving.com
www.norfolknaturalliving.com
Pages 10; 11 a; 22 ar; 28 l; 29 r; 31; 40; 45; 61; 62–63; 65; 68 c; 126–127; 154.

Sophie Rowell
@cotedefolk
www.cotedefolk.com
Pages 4 l; 25 r; 39 l; 42; 43; 51; 54 l; 54 ar; 56 r; 58; 69 ar; 70 r; 72–73; 104–105; 140–141; 167 ar.

Paul West
@consideredthings
Pages 44 r; 55; 57 r; 82; 92; 93 l; 93 c; 106–107; 108–111; 134–135; 138–139; 148; 150–151; 166; 167 l; 173.

ACKNOWLEDGMENTS

I'm so grateful to have produced my eleventh book, so my heartfelt thanks goes to my publishers Ryland Peters & Small for commissioning my Heritage idea. Producing a book is a process that involves a huge team, from all at RPS to all the wonderful home owners, designers and craftspeople who have agreed to be part of it and whose creativity has been hugely inspiring. THANK YOU ALL SO MUCH.

Rachel Whiting, thank you for your dedication to producing gorgeous images and your eagerness to capture the perfect light. We always have so much fun together even on the busiest days. Thanks for being a lovely friend.

Finally thanks to my family – Mum and Dad and my wonderful husband Dave, for all his design and DIY projects in our house.

Love Selina

SOURCES

PAINT

Heritage by Dulux
duluxheritage.co.uk
The Heritage range consists of 112 shades inspired by historical colours.

Edward Bulmer
edwardbulmerpaint.co.uk
Heritage paint colours and eco-friendly paint specialists.

Farrow & Ball
farrow-ball.com
A British manufacturer of paints and wallpapers largely based upon historic colour palettes.

Little Greene
littlegreene.com
High-quality paints and wallcoverings plus a heritage collection in association with The National Trust.

The Pickleson Paint Co
picklesonpaint.com
A sustainable paint company offering water-based, eco-friendly paint.

Mylands
mylands.com
Established in 1884, Mylands is Britain's oldest family-run paint manufacturer.

SOFT FURNISHINGS

Anna Jeffreys
Annajeffreys.co.uk
Pretty printed linen and wallpaper.

Claremont fabrics
claremontfurnishing.com
Specialist textiles and trimmings.

Designers Guild
designersguild.com
Bold and colourful fabrics and wallpaper designs by Tricia Guild.

GP & J Baker
gpjbaker.com
Historic designs produced by the holder of a Royal Warrant.

Inchyra
inchyra.com
Timeless fabrics and accessories from the foothills of the Scottish Highlands.

Ottoline
ottoline.co.uk
Fabric and wallpaper designs as well as cushions and lampshades.

Pippa Blacker Interiors
pippablackerinteriors.co.uk
Designer and creator of beautiful soft furnishings, curtains, blinds and interior design schemes.

Projektityyny
projektityyny.com
Gingham, wide stripe and embroidered linen tablecloths, cushions, quilts and napkins.

Susan Deliss
susandeliss.com
Susan designs her own range of fabrics and braids for upholstery, curtains and interior decoration and has a small and highly regarded interior design practice.

Sylvia & Margot
sylviaandmargot.com
Made-to-order hand-illustrated and lino-printed textiles and wallpapers.

Zoffany
zoffany.sandersondesigngroup.com
Traditional damasks and velvets.

WALLCOVERINGS

Cole & Son
cole-and-son.com
Producing luxury wallpapers and fabrics since 1875.

The English Panelling Company
englishpanellingcompany.co.uk
Bespoke panelling to add character to interiors.

Lewis & Wood
lewisandwood.co.uk
Beautiful and unusual fabrics and wallpapers.

Morris & Co
www.morrisandco.sandersondesigngroup.com
Original wallpaper and fabric designs by William Morris.

Soane Britain
soane.co.uk
Designers and makers of furniture, rattan, upholstery, lighting, fabric and wallpaper.

FURNITURE

Another Country
anothercountry.com
Contemporary furniture and home accessories.

Drew Pritchard Antiques
drewpritchard.co.uk.
Decorative antiques.

The Dormy House
dormyhouse.com
Furniture, storage and soft furnishings.

Ercol
ercol.com
A family firm that has been producing well-designed and made contemporary furniture since 1920.

George Smith
georgesmith.com
Luxury and hand-crafted upholstered furniture made by experienced makers.

Howe London
howelondon.com
A collection of new hand-crafted furniture plus sublime antiques.

Matthew Cox
matthewcox.com
Made-to-measure furniture alongside carefully chosen antiques.

Pinch Design
pinchdesign.com
Quiet, elegant contemporary furniture that fits perfectly in a heritage interior.

LIGHTING

Anglepoise
anglepoise.com
Quintessentially British lighting brand with origins dating back to 1932.

Jamb
jamb.co.uk
Antique and reproduction fireplaces, lighting and more.

Original BTC
originalbtc.com
Familiar, traditional utilitarian shapes at accessible prices.

Rosi de Ruig
rosi-de-ruig.myshopify.com
Handmade paper lampshades and elegant, practical table lamps.

Tom Dixon
tomdixon.net
Contemporary lighting, accessories and furniture that will be the antiques of tomorrow.

KITCHENS & JOINERY

Block House Build
blockhousebuild.com
London-based building and project management company focusing on beautiful joinery.

deVOL
devolkitchens.co.uk
Bespoke makers of
handmade kitchens and
simple, beautiful furniture.

Plain English
plainenglishdesign.co.uk
Bespoke wooden kitchens
made with an immaculate
attention to detail.

British Standard Cupboards
britishstandardcupboards.
co.uk
A sister brand to Plain
English producing wooden
kitchens at a more
affordable price point.

Neptune
neptune.com
Beautifully made furniture,
kitchens, lighting, home
decor and more.

Thorncomb Design
thorncombe.co.uk
Renovation, joinery
and bespoke panelling.

Wickes
wickes.co.uk
Suppliers of quality home
improvement products and
budget-friendly kitchens.

**ACCESSORIES FOR
HOME AND GARDEN**
Daylesford
daylesford.com
Organic food plus home
and garden shops.

Ebay
ebay.com
Online marketplace to seek
out antique furniture and
vintage accessories.

Etsy
etsy.com
A marketplace for vintage
furniture, fabrics, lighting
and decorative pieces.

Le Petit Jardin
www.le-petit-jardin.com
Gorgeous garden and
homeware shop, supplying
stylish gardeners and home
makers in and around the
lovely spa town of Tunbridge
Wells, UK.

Liberty London
Regent Street
London W1B 5AH
libertylondon.com
Discover a full range of luxury
fabrics, designer furniture,
stylish homewares and unique
curios at London's favourite
heritage department store.

Matilda Goad
matildagoad.com
Scalloped rattan
lampshades, decorative
ceramics, ribbed and
hexagon colourful candles
and tole planters.

Petersham Nurseries
Church Lane
Petersham Road
TW10 7AB
petershamnurseries.com
A place of beauty and an
emporium of interior and
garden accessories.

Will & Yates
104–106 High Street
Deal
Kent CT14 6EE
willandyates.com
Original paintings, prints,
ceramics, antiques and soft
furnishings.

**HERITAGE
INSPIRATIONS**
Coalport China Museum
ironbridge.org.uk

English Heritage
english-heritage.org.uk

National Trust
nationaltrust.org.uk

Preservation Directory
Preservationdirectory.com
A directory of historic
societies and preservation
organizations in the US.

Royal Horticultural Society
rhs.org.uk

*Weald and Downland Living
Museum*
wealddown.co.uk

**STYLING/DESIGN
CONCEPT BOARDS**
*Soft pinks & earthy tones
(page 33)*
Little Green Paint chart;
Stitch in Pale Plaster by
Damson & Slate from
Alexander Maverick;
Fruit wallpaper and Ruskin
Linen both by Morris & Co.;
Beauclerc Stripe in Natural
Rose by Inchyra; Wes
gingham napkin in blush
by Projektityyny; Lavender
Path linen, Arabella, and
English Oak in Red on
Natural, all by Pippa Blacker
Interiors; Jasper linen and
Luxe Linen both from The
Dormy House; Quartz Velvet
Parchment by Zoffany;
Pentle Herringbone Alder
Sisal Carpet from Country
Living Collection at
Carpetright; hand-painted
foxglove card from
gennakoomenshop.com;
Tarte Tan and Sunday
Brown paint swatches from
Pickleson; gingham fabric
and printed card from
Hobbycraft; crockery and
moss napkin image by
Neptune.

*Fresh greens & ochre
(page 37)*
Millefleur wallpaper in
Garden from National Trust
Papers II at Little Greene;
natural check napkin from

Daylesford; mustard linen
napkin from Zara Home;
Couronne aged linen in Fern
Green by Inchrya; Laurel
linen in Sunshine by Anna
Jeffreys; Brera Lino in
Cocoa by Designers Guild;
Quartz Velvet in Gold by
Zoffany; English Oak in
Green on Natural by Pippa
Blacker Interiors; Ruskin
Manilla Linen by Morris &
Co; Pentle Tigers Eye sisal
carpet from Country Living
Collection at Carpetright;
Farrow & Ball paint chart;
Wes gingham cushion in
mustard from Projektityyny;
Lemon gingham card from
Hobbycraft; vintage ribbon
from a vintage market.

*Rich blues & sea greens
(page 41)*
Helene wallpaper in Ochre
Blue by Anna Jeffreys;
Meredith wallpaper in
Blue from the Coromandel
Collection and Marguerite
wallpaper from Les Rêves
collection both by Nina
Campbell; Marigold wallpaper
in Wedgwood by Morris &
Co; Sunflowers linen in Arts
and Crafts Blue by Sylvia
& Margot; Artisan Weave
in Sourdough, House Linen
in Olive, Vintage Linen in
Moss, House Linen, Beaulieu
Leather in Honey all Love
your Home; Quartz Velvet in
Chalk by Zoffany; Millbrook
in Dove by GP & J Baker;
Birch Loop Pile carpet in
Hedgehog from Country
Living range at Carpertright;
Rattan wallcovering in
Off-White by Arte; Edward
Bulmer paint chart; sample
pot of Blue Toile paint from
Bejamin Moore; for a similar
striped fabric, try Romo.

INDEX

Page numbers in *italic* refer to the illustrations